A winter of remarkable oranges descended. It was an apparition of first succulence and sections tender and bursting, charged and sweet, soaked with harvesting life. It had its own prism. Loaves, rum, tea and brandy joined that university and made providence no purse could hold or say.

Through the aureola of its season, a transporting, a dirvish jig-and-reel of desire carried days away. From groves and loaves winter brought turbulents and paler breaths; bold chromatics; loss and gain; salt, smoke and rain; gods and puzzles of all sorts; port and cheese; trees with old eyes and whorled leaves; partridge and cranberry, Labrador tea; fiddle, rhythm-sticks and woodwind; cats, gables and starved lips; celestial charts and rumouring; stone-cradles and required paddles; scarves, guitars, remembrance and barnacles; child and age; lyric and tragic page; machinery and divinity; sparrows, mice and bone; conquistadors, daggers, dust and rust; home, sun and starlight fealty; magi and wintered-eye; full-aria and blasphemy; guns and wineskins; masks and bookends; draped cloth and absence; logic cobbled with eloquence; almanacs and governance; endowments and deliverance and old ghosts curious upon the shoulder.

The bacchanal oranges and loaves of winter,
through weather and the hour,
brought the pilgrim nearer
his slow-approaching flower

Medieval Light

I was born into a medieval light
Read by the snake-hiss of a lamp;
a shiver and hiss which spread
parables upon the book and bowed head

The house was a story
beneath alps of snow
Magnified mightily, three-fold
we were, where life got told

The triptych of
birth, love and death was lit
and kept by a mantled-tongue of gas
A switch lobotomized that past

2.
Staring through this winter night
the bright page is marked
by a beaten path between two worlds:
the mantled-gas; the electric pearl

Boyd Warren Chubbs

The Winter of Remarkable Oranges

I follow my imagination, that true lamp, pure luminary, maker of fallen and regained worlds.

BREAKWATER

BREAKWATER

100 Water Street • P.O. Box 2188 • St. John's • NL • A1C 6E6
www.breakwaterbooks.com

National Library of Canada Cataloguing in Publication

Chubbs, Boyd Warren, 1955-
       Winter of remarkable oranges / Boyd Warren Chubbs.

Poems.
ISBN 1-55081-207-6 (bound).—ISBN 1-55081-208-4 (pbk.)
I. Title.

PS8555.H8W55 2004   C811'.54   C2004-900749-1

© 2004 Boyd Warren Chubbs

"I Met A Saint on Coronation Street" appeared in
*The Backyards of Heaven: An Anthology of Contemporary Poetry
from Ireland and Newfoundland and Labrador* (2003)

All images by the Author
Author's photograph by Ray Fennelly
Design & Layout: Rhonda Molloy

The Canada Council | Le Conseil des Arts
for the Arts | du Canada

We acknowledge the financial support of
The Canada Council for the Arts for our publishing activities.

Canada

We acknowledge the financial support of the Government of
Canada through the Book Publishing Industry Development
Program (BPIDP) for our publishing activities.

I Brought My Stories

I brought my stories and worries
to the electric city
Except to pigeons and rare moons
they weren't currency

Blinded and rattled;
repelling collapse in the weather and wear
I suffered through pronouncements
and maps to various havens and heavens proffered here

Endowments and deliverance;
the full life, sated and wise,
were all for the taking it was said
through this new and tempting noise

I muttered and marled upon
the Hill. Passed limousines. Into the pub
at the sight of loss and gain
I remembered then the rub:

in the revelry of the room
fulfillment's a plate of food
long-pursued, rapidly consumed
Hunger has already entered the womb

Song and a Golden String

When I returned the angel had gone
but there, written in the new fall
she'd left me a song
singing, find some small water to bless
or a single leaf
in this winter of remarkable oranges
I leave you and leave you with your wonderment
between this midnight
and a distant continent

I folded the Comfortable Words into my coat,
into my head and pulled my eyes tight
imagining for the guitar, her song by note
and knew misery, too, must have a keel
of submerged mirth—
the light-and-dark wheel
With my bucket of stars I started to sing:
she left me by Glynmill Pond
with song and a golden string

Words With My Old Friend, Mr. Ryall

I'm a horse among first grass and clover;
a salmon tracing a new river;
a rose; a berry;
language bracing through
a traveler with an arcane list:
to die by drink is to fly by water;
on earth there can't be a Holy Father;
love isn't a blob on a specimen glass;
everything is equal, at last,
when you become the fulcrum;
we are vessels on a string;
sufficient for torment is wisdom;
the looming, obtuse-angled cliff
teaches gravity of passage
to the grotto or windshift

Have you been to heaven, lately
Oh, great vistas to learn your wings
The lord is tongue-tied and
the quiet, quietly sing
My wish? That the lyric and tragic
elevate this place to devise
a bright path to reach through
dim days of skies

The rise and fall I know
stumbling to achieve transition
Note it all. Find the startle in
all ephemera, that raw surrealism
See! I wear all colours-
black has consumed the prism

The Stranger's House

1.
There's a house on the precipice of a continent
Its door's a curtain and window a bare frame
Birds, dogs, come and go
with rain, sun and songs. No calendars;
no long deed marking the land
Baptisms, funerals; the lost and found
share a room with
sea and thunder in sound and resound
All that's been
remains layered there, imaged
as tracings on onion-skin

There's a barren of berries;
groves and orchards; loaves and fish
brilliant upon the counter
There's machinery and divinity
and love, offered through a burgundy rose
and ribs of a shrub, and a turbulent brook
where trouters kneel to kiss the hook
A full grape wires the wine
and one, on whose head whole autumns live,
lights the long room with fire

A meandering path links it to the world,
a path, fabric unfurled

2.
Who lives there?
Who carries the lamp
when we are asleep or absent?

As the light weaves, what light it leaves:
upon, within the house above the rocks;
beneath Leda and Jupiter;
in the middle of everywhere with
weather striking clocks
And the circling echo brews
marriage of old and new

In This Summered-December
Read Everything and Remember

Rain above Trepassey started from a drop
probably lifted from this side of the place,
from the face of a Calvert trout-pond
or from a sea-lop then up through rainbows,
settling into the trades one day
joining, over Cape St. Francis, others drifted that way
A crop of weather made and remade
as it carried, shifted, lossed and gained
in the circumnavigation above and upon
gardens, lips, marriages, warriors, nations
starved for rain

There by the store where you lean with your book,
in this summered-December
read everything and remember,
nod at what's passing and know why
Handshakes of yesterday make and remake
There's a cloud of brooding-velvet in the sky
turning its steeples and domes this way
Its limbs are winged translucence. It brings,
over St. Patrick's, a wake of fired water
upon revellers, cats, gables and age
As it passes catch a drop,
a remembrance and mark for your page

McCarthy Returns to Long's Hill

I stand where a turbulent had been
A lithe breath is set upon the sills,
calico of summer brought to a winter-merciful;
bringing stillness to the curbs
where Mr. Slaney tidies what's been disturbed

The Premier's with his Cabinet
The Miner's with his Drill
I'm here in the warmth
of the shawl of Long's Hill

A bold chromatic pulled aside the clouds
The ridge revels with purpose and talk
A child emerges and begins to walk
toward pigeons round with bread
the light wheeling on their darting heads

The Banker's with his Money
The Hunter's with his Kill
I'm here with eternity-
the shawl of Long's Hill

After bare absence I see her,
the head that drinks the sun
striding through a corona of lund
Nothing can extend the blood of a season
like the return of a friend

The Vintner's with his Aging-cask
The Harvester's at his Mill
I remain, I will remain
with the shawl of Long's Hill

In Ferryland

The holy grail's on every table,
hands mighty around each life
Extra leafs are fitted for the arriving
In from woodlots, pawnshops and excursions
we gather, the room roguish with laughter

Through the Festival, when Imagination is Supreme,
dreaming of wings and tongues, becoming one
with air and rungs of heaven,
diviners drink from the fountained-earth;
fables are propelled by renaissance;
chained and unchained are the weightless,
the floor somewhere below; the broken are able
to follow long-steeped dance
The assembled wonder at lightness and ease
Beautifully-ageless, we've become as syllables
from the first responding drum

But gravity ensures descent
Though full-fire of the sublime,
of sun and starlight fealty
gilds a day well-spent
one shout from a collector's mouth;
one blooded-scrape of the razor across the face;
one word announcing time is dear,
boots would burn the floor
and weather would wail through the door

We'll remain in this heightened room
and swallow, follow blaze of birth
the news tipping from the grail
I tend the glow from the slow lamp
in the wintered-eye of the magi,
where the summer iris is stamped

A Winter's Night

To say that one is less or one is more
is to lose both peace and war

Sparrows perish with the condor;
condors with mice next door;
mice with a leaf strangled by my window
long past November. A wind
took it to the ground. That wind
reached Middle Cove, got swallowed by a lund
The lund went and got lost by a grotto
where visitors, a storm of them,
pounded gates, grass and stones,
stones equal to dandelions,
massacred in sunlight and starlight,
starlight perishing before the sun again

Regimes will burn
for the slaughtering of dreams
Supplanters, too, cede to dagger and dust
like conquistadors, lifting the brutal as light,
become rust

Old Christmas Night: Midnight

Again the flash-and-flair thundered by the aperture
its blaze, upon wishbones and children,
starved and gone; trees are returning to woods

After twelve gluttonous stations from Eve to Eve,
across pearled snow, breath is frozen tight
by a clarion note pronouncing lament

On this advent, with a book by lamplight,
I read of a vastness where an exile stood
Turning there in a silence-dome he received

sweet water, bread, almond and blossoms
Not thunder and thunder's blaze
just small wonders heralding mysterious days

Report from a Foreign Country

Government has no sleep or death
Doors swing, there, on mysterious hinges
The sensible, entering, can't retrace their steps

Robins will find the worm on the spring return
Quilts worn thin are stitched new
Wire is a peculiar bugle and tuba flag-pole burn

Curious roam hills and maps, days into years wed
The bold are young and old
Love tangles much as it ever did

Boundaries of the home remain
Dogs scratch and store a bone
Idlers come and go, sizing the rain

The mystified are elevated
The needle in the glass is a trapeze of forecasts
Visitors leave saying the country's gated

A country is a puzzling and grievous notion
The flag is both forecast and anthem
To be is desperation and devotion

To a Winter Traveler

1.
To find your return
tie a scarf around the common juniper
A little distance,
wrap another around the low rough
On the path imagine
the abundance queuing:
black crowberry, partridge and cranberry;
twinflower, lambkill, sheep and bog laurel;
and although you won't see,
sweet gale and Labrador tea

These are heartbreaker hills
In the lesser-light
trees will seem to be huddled seekers
with weather-eyes and whorled leaves
gone to leather
There are ghosts, curious upon your shoulder
and the air isn't colder
More can be said between
living and dead

Through this snow, wind, scruff and roar
you are welcome through the communion door,
to a rail where the cup is full
from a brook beneath your knees
You are a flame
and your name will be said
with Kingman's Cove, Grey Islands and Bareneed;
Troake, Norman and Penashue;
O'Brien, Terriak and Cumby;
Old Perlican, Lac Cunard and Little Heart's Ease

2.
Winter lives in the nape
Pull back its frosted shape
and along the underside of its parapets
look at spring preparing flint

Here, in this bowstring season
many times love dies
You've seen
its death never arrives

Through His Half-day; Half-night

Rain, shifting the vane,
drifts upon a buyer of manuscripts and candlesticks;
maps and nonsense; upon his zeal,
unreal thirst of zeal and tricks
He's gathering everything,
anything the weather brings

And all that the weather brings
he stuffs in boxes, cars and boats
Leaving nothing, he fills pockets
with moss and artichokes
Finding a shingle a beginner lost
he wraps it in cloth,
binds it with string, stores it for keeping
Years pass beneath this overcast

The overcast condenses upon his non-sleeping
He gathers, stacks and layers
filling cellars and stairs,
cups, tubs, attic
Loads every board
Hoarding is its own reward
he's heard from somewhere
in diminishing candlelight,
piling and counting through
his half-day; half-night

Coastal Collectors

I remember tall shapes and voices, proper in doorways
upon stageheads, their purses full and tight
for muzzle-loaders and clocks;
chromed-tables, chairs, mirrors and fine pots
Just a clutter in your kitchen, isn't it Mrs.
those old guns and faded dishes
And the lamps, sure new ones have a steady light
and those dressers and jars
new ones have a luster like stars
up and down day or night
A dollar here, a fiver there,
for promises, lies and fears
the rare and dear disappeared

To the gunnels and out to sea
tides pulled their dark shapes against the sun
By stoves, by tea,
talk of riches dulled against enormity

Then, now, and always they move:
Dig the basement before the paper's dry
Bless the land and sea with your industry
Don't lift a battle cry
it'll crucify prosperity
Here's a bit of hay; here's a bit of clover
Here's a promise. Now, roll over

The Vendor Brings Heroin and Violins

The vendor brings heroin and violins;
guns and wineskins;
dramatic masks for bookends
He's eager-bright with his reasons

The legislator makes laws and maps;
reverence with messianic deliverance;
tone and intone of gall and governance
He weaves and swells in a reasoned dance

Gobble paper but mourn the tree's descent;
revere light then repel its brilliance
with draped cloth or absence
Logic's cobbled with eloquence

Well-seasoned, well-mannered is reason
But it's a treason to the soul
to proffer freedom while fire, the galvanizing angel
is chained in an earthly leg-hold

From the Steeple of 'The Kirk'

Who's mad? Who's bright?
Who's far? Who's near?
Who was she standing there?
Who said right! when
parts were ripped from here?

Not the finish of belief, a question
Some, dead, haven't gone past the reef
A nord'easter, the width of it,
shows them signaling,
lights above the lops on these brief evenings

Recalling a Midnight

In this room, close as bullets,
I've killed a moth. An accidental wrist
struck its leap, robbed that twist
once a frantic-strange

Under the lamp,
folded and brown the moth goes
and dies upon notes,
a letter to mother about summer,
about hybrids, enigmas in August
and now, how a moth grows

Red Shoes in Winter

No sparks from them
Won't hear them strike the floor
From near or far
won't catch their rhythm
Not possible to touch them,
to find their width or make
Won't see a pair
to gauge their fineness by
Can't tell when they'll appear

But, for me, when the chill in all things
brings dark upon the land, sea and wings;
when my home collapses
from too much collapsing,
there they are in
a waltz that never begins
or ends through fluent center-
red shoes in winter

I Knew a Man

1.

I knew a man, a youthful man
He had all kinds of plans yesterday
with gods of Placentia Bay songs
ruling his island mouth

We encountered in a mall
where I'd gone for a book
by a poet I needed most
That proud and tall man's face
had become a shroud

Trouble found him on a troubled night:
placed a Siberia through his ribs;
caused the oil on his gifted tongue
to crud and crack and
his sense to come undone;
dropped his voice to dark weather;
slaved a confession;
shaded lids over his bright eyes
Canals of his body
closed to navigation

2.

That long-ago morning lives as signpost and speech
bold lettering on the will and walk
I reach for bread and his words are in the head
I meet and talk in the bunker, on the barrens,
and everywhere
his solemn, broken face
breaks the sky

3.

Distance between days is perilous
A set-pattern of sun, moon and rest
can't guarantee flawlessness
Processions by bullwhips or spaceships;
Christian or Heathen in
full-aria or blaspheme,
upon the earth's fire and sigh
in birth-clothes stagger by

Last Apples on a Night Tree

I've looked at fields
sown for carnivals, not food
I've been to a mansion without cupboards
and two lovers swayed there,
last apples on a night tree
And I wonder at the Olympian distance
between maker and vendor
In the stunted, contorted tamarack
I see places carrying all worry on the back

Everything keeps the world
and the world keeps everything
Temptations on every string
Everywhere tormenters and no wind
to blow the mould off them
Birthplace alone not enough
to claim a home
Ours not being the only life
we can't be the only death

To love or not to love;
to ignore the genie or succumb
In a repulsion a magnifier finds blessing:
midnight brilliant on a wrecking ball;
an exquisite hook ripping through a cod's skull
The study chills, fills and distills
like the providing,
providential and ruthless sea
Everything's a strange ambiguity

There's a Wide Ribbon

1.
There's a wide ribbon from my bed
looping toward a fine glow over Nepean
over and through spread of winter
and east, farther east, in accord with the sight
of late day; young night
It's a sober startle, an eerie roadway
diminuative and massive undulations
above a yeast of nations
with prayers and bright players of woodwind,
fiddle, rhythm-sticks and you
high-stepping the long, winding and layered place-
stations imbibing your face

2.
But this room, this mall of walls,
exhales the sour glue of the new
I'm oppressed by its nothingness
Fresh from the clouds and reefs
your kindness upon the sheets I need,
that ether; that aril from the sea

3.
The vision grows less
The mall of walls enlarges

A Late Remembrance

Remember the crane? Seems just yesterday
its elegance across low-tide
elevated the marsh, already citied and dressed
with yellow-reed and the plover's quickness

The electrified-blue of that Tuesday,
inverted into that place and folded
like Provence light,
became a parable upon your swimmer's face

In lieu of a diamond or ruby glow
I offer that memory,
that treasure, its resonance
your birthday's undertow

Child and Age

The universe is the size of my skull
Time, width of the wall I write upon
All items on the list
the equal of a kiss:
sky of home in my head;
a capstan pulling providence from its bed;
suite of songs, haulin' songs, across the reef
fish, hymns and bakeapple leaf

Child and Age share the same page
Hear what the birds say:
same wings, beak and claws
raised by this divinity of laws
Within this body, though a diminishing fire,
I'm sustained by a kiss, the first desire

Travel Guide

Far hills, those exotics,
won't fill your canvas or travel sack
Anyway, the trek is interminable,
dark by the time you'd dive
And those hills won't fill your pockets
or unravel the tangled string you bring
They'll keep their magazine distance
You'll travel, not arrive

Far hills are no more
Too long gone, wake and gather yourself
Upon the return you'll stare where
your hills had been
And you'll stumble and wonder
who could have taken them

Rocks are Loose

1.

Rocks are loose even when they're not
I know this, without knowing rocks
An owl tried to stop
but the mouse flew free because of a rolling rock

A house made of mountains, a solid height,
gave up its mind in an avalanched-night
'Runnin the Goat' upon a cliff
dancers lost their legs when sea-stones split

Though winter made a full-belly of the barrens
beneath I could see shifting shapes;
collapsing cairns

2.

From here to Nain
weather has loosened the stone-cradles
and you haven't turned the required paddles
or boots or wings
critical to how such a journey begins

with words, words upon their cross of play
bright at night; hidden by day

Begin where the ancients stood
how they knew to follow rocks
tongue-and-groove with wood

Anno Domini 2001:
The Genesis All Years Become

News through the screen seems
to be a sound from a single broom,
one fashioned in an atomic room
There in the undermaking a reverberation,
a grim bell equal with the times
moves in the groove of a curl;
upon wooden, painted globes of this world;
upon barnacles in a graveyard-marine;
on rust upon barnacles
where opera and dolls had been;
upon scarves, wharves, guitars and bowls;
upon monocles, bicycles, barbers, scullers and wheels;
through futures; through a wardrobe of fields and
through the old and cold doorways
where no one can go,
a profiting tongue in the undertow

Peace and grace have no profit to give
You or I upon a podium or wall,
braving winter and delusion
where we love and live,
would be driven to the kennels
for breaking the rhythm; driven to the kennels
for altering the view of the few

The Bird's Nest

It was a tough drizzle
It was fog in the bone
Breath was a train's tongue
meandering home

I found a broken nest
on the river's bib
Fallen near the tide
bare, skeletal ribs

lay stark-still on the mud
Damp was her day
I stood, spoke and nodded
at her brief parade

Years, We've Made, Can Only Tell

Count years to know youth or age?
More profitable counting words
to make a page

A boy is afire with rumours and fun
slows in a quiet room
rolling a small stone under his tongue
Tracing a pattern from a celestial chart
he stares outside at a close night and
places a book over his heart

And there's one, who's lived seven times more
Snow's a blizzard upon his head
He approachs his house and stands by the door
Face to the sky he begins a tune
Neighbours point and pass
He's there 'til dark and sings to the moon

Jennifer is younger than Megan, nearly,
and by their side
Jim is younger than the stars, barely
making age in prayer and song
Years we've made can only tell
we've been and gone

Gifts and Allegories

1.
Nothing is still
Nothing is without the constant swirl,
the anchored chaotic
in an invisible world

2.
There's more than one source of light
There's no constant proportion. The narrative
is incomplete. Time is as varied
as the face of a cloud; a rock; water's motion

Angeling: Poem for Oslo

Castlines and salmon runs are sipped
as history over lips
Particulars of water and weather said
with a bell's intensity. Face and eyes
are coals in the fire-bed

In the telling there is no nowhere
and no middle these tellers have known
Everywhere is somewhere
Rivers and steadies are gables of home
No far or near. Just there

And never is there nothing
The filament strikes from the wrist to the pool,
to a sound, a shape, a notion,
an urgency, a need, a salmon scale,
the river announcing to the ocean

The Amaranth

Throw away greater or better
Care for the imaginary flower
or folds of a Belgian's fetter
Post long-promised letters
as a delicious end of day;
as a drink to the hour

Keep wonderment. Let neighbours be
centered in brilliant impossibility
Beneath sun or moon
shakers of snow are a sublime adagio
All gifts sought had balsamed finery-
were trees in a Christmas lot

It's devastation to rate
the tide's push and pull
Grading can't escape the inescapeable-
existence is untranslateable

I Met a Saint

I met a saint on Coronation Street
against snow, blackened in April
the remains of salt, smoke and rain
He said, there against all the stuff and sun,
sizing the day against the porch:

> There are several arctics
> and several americas;
> several neighbourhoods and several ways
> to gods and puzzles of all sorts

Among blackened snow, the street cat,
a Labrador and early crow, he said:

> Can't find a church
> to record my miracles
> Can't find a friend
> who's heard of oracles

The crow found a half-loaf;
the cat scratched and groomed the Labrador
I pressed one hand upon the membrane
between night and day
and stared at the man by his door:

Don't make a city
where brooks run dry
and don't go without leaving
love where it dies

Light enlarges and the crow has flown
The cat purrs on. The Labrador licks his parts.
I turn to leave this stunning reprieve
and hear before I depart:

Sir, I'm a saint with saintly ways
But no one records my miracles these days
After the melt I'll lie with gulls, lichens and locks
in the passed-by mansion of the sea rocks

At that, I pause but there's no more
Just a slow and rattled closing of his door

Rowan

I've seen a gift
in the smallest shift of a cat;
read one in the lore
of the brave Almanac and
heard one from a young tree, saying
'I missed you wide and way back'

Three Poems in April, for E.W.

1.

Lower the figure from his wind-and-cold cross
Thaw his limbs, ruin and lungs
Let him move as poems do
pilgrims on the road to loving tongues

I searched lanes and marginal wharves
to find coins and a stove for his stations
For him, like Job, I went mourning without the sun
and stood up to cry in the congregations

It will be, always the brilliant bright
of arsenals dull
against the original light
from Dante and Michelangelo
or the boy, there, feeding pigeons off Wildegrave
Auguries of bloom for the poorly-brave

2.

Neighbours, are your sabres in scabbards;
knives in sheaths;
all weapons, brutal and clever
benign and buried beneath?

I pray the spines of your books
aren't dying as window-props
or perishing on the floor as
all-season doorstops

Have you noticed ravens nesting by our windows
in the tall, starved pine, marking their stay
in this earlier Sabbath,
barking and wheeling through turbulent grey

I can't function apart from their private nation;
I stare and stare at their frantic creation

3.
Look and wait for everything
I hear feet
slow-dragged through
near and farther streets

Who's guarding the unguardable room
where the passioned dropped after he'd been lynched?
Will a breath blow into his embalmed mouth
and unfold him into magnificence?
Will a pale moon see him as astrallite,
from a modest quiver a drenched power
through cirrus and nimbus, an arc of archetype
exclaiming the perfection of the hour?

Will that flight be the essential star
to galvanize us, now seeing that far?

The Passing of Michael O'Neill (1935-2003)

1.
The first brace was from a question:
'Have you met my son Paul?'
He spoke of great trouble on the road
There among the sweep, load and
ruck of Duckworth Street
I knew all were Paul, disciple son

I drew the red cliff of his face,
the sea and thespian contortions of its run,
ten times
Ten times more
wouldn't be sufficient
to show cigarettes pulled to his lips like peppermint

2.
In the bare chapel
one Sister reads of wisdom;
the other, of merciful rest
For the devoted and sparse assemblage
the Priest attempts
his script for enlightenment

No personal words. No throngs
for a later wake of testimonials and songs
His form rolled in and now out
to the Avondale Assumption gate
No pallbearers; no one who knew him
to carry him and know his weight

Juno and Catherine

In Flatrock a piper begins
Through trees something rare
plays upon the laden and bare
Old ones told how to hear that sound
those dense and intense syllables
of lament or celebrational coming 'round

Piped from the same lungs
and sturdy as a winter's night goes on
differing melodies lift a startling song
Beneath constellations, a dance-drenched mass,
the blended air is a stardust stair
where two meteors cross and pass

Caravans and caravans go hypnotic ways
one departing; one coming in
through a high door on a fine hinge
The passage slumps upon the skin and sleeve
Morning merges with blueberries and blood
The piper's done and takes leave

finis

Author's Note

I'm grateful to the *Canada Council for the Arts* and the *Newfoundland and Labrador Arts Council* for financial support. I thank Florence Donaway and Scott Strong for their close and valued reading of an earlier draft of this work; Rhonda Molloy for her fine flourishing design abilities; my publisher Clyde Rose, of Breakwater Books who has provided a freedom which enables me to bring my books to full realization, from the beginning of words to all accompanying imagery.

The twelve thematic images through this work are from an exhibition *I Make A Covenant With My Eyes*, drawings based upon selections from the Book of Job and exhibited at the Christina Parker Gallery in St. John's in October 2003 and which are now in a private collection.

The text is set in Perpetua, a font from the early 1900s and based on stone-cutter's alphabets.

www.ingramcontent.com/pod-product-compliance
Lightning Source LLC
Chambersburg PA
CBHW060557100426

42742CB00013B/2592